...Extreme Pets...

LIZARD

Deborah Chancellor

W
FRANKLIN WATTS
LONDON • SYDNEY

First published in 2007 by Franklin Watts
338 Euston Road, London NW1 3BH

Franklin Watts Australia
Level 17/207 Kent Street
Sydney NSW 2000

Editors: Rachel Tonkin and Julia Bird
Designer: Proof Books
Picture researcher: Diana Morris
Consultant: Mitch Price

Picture credits:
Arco Images/Alamy: 20, 25; Niall Benvie/Nature PL: 28; Carol Buchanan: 23; Stephen Dalton/NHPA: 26;
Michael & Patricia Fogden/Corbis: 24; John Fowler: 16; John Gaffen/White Windmill Photography: 22;
Les Gibbon/Alamy: front cover, 1; Juniors Bildarchive/Alamy: 9; Richard Levine Photography: 6;
Jean Preston-Mafham/Premaphotos: 21; David Manning/Papilio: 19; Teresa Mayer: 12;
Buddy Mays: 9; Natural Visions Picture Library: 4; Alf Jacob Nilsen/Bioquatic Photo: 13, 15;
David A. Northcott/Corbis: 9b, 18; Photofusion/Alamy: 29; Jeremy Piper/epa/Corbis: 27;
Jonathan Plant/Alamy: 11.

With thanks to Alice Kohler and Hazel, and Hazel's pet
bearded dragon, Norman.

Every attempt has been made to clear copyright.
Should there be any inadvertent omission please
apply to the publisher for rectification.

A CIP catalogue record for this book
is available from the British Library

ISBN: 978 0 7496 7063 4

Dewey Classification: 639.3'95

Printed in China

Franklin Watts is a division of Hachette Children's Books.

Contents

Do you want a lizard?

Lizards are reptiles, which means they hatch from eggs and are covered in scales. Reptiles are cold-blooded animals so they cannot control their own body temperature. They rely on outside heat or cold to do this. They live in a variety of habitats, from deserts to rainforests. Some species of lizards can be kept as pets.

Good pets

Lizards can make good pets because they are fascinating to watch and not too messy. They are quiet pets, and smaller species don't take up much space. They also don't affect people who have asthma or fur allergies.

Hard work

All pet lizards need special care. Their equipment is expensive and can be complicated to set up, and your lizard may eat very unusual food. You must be sure you and your family have the time, money and enthusiasm to keep your lizard healthy and happy.

Lizards are cold-blooded, so they need to warm themselves in the sun's heat. This is called 'basking'.

Health risk

Lizards are carriers of bacteria, including salmonella. This bacterial infection is dangerous for children under five and for pregnant, sick or old people. You shouldn't keep lizards if you live with anyone who fits this description. If you do keep lizards, always use strict hygiene when you feed and hold them, and when cleaning out their tanks.

Do your research

Not all lizards are the same, and you need to work out which species will suit you best. Find out how big your chosen lizard will grow, and how long it will live. Discover what it needs to stay healthy. Find out about its temperament and behaviour – for example, will it mind being held, and is it active by day or night? You also need to find a vet who can treat your lizard if it gets ill.

Close to home

Most lizards live in hot places, but some smaller species live in cooler, temperate climates, for example the common lizard in the UK.

Holiday cover

If you want to get a lizard as a pet, you will need to find someone to look after it when your family goes on holiday. This person will have to understand the heating, lighting and feeding needs of your lizard, and be prepared to keep it in their own home. Never leave your lizard alone at home without the care it needs to stay alive.

Questions & Answers

✳ **What is the most popular pet lizard?**
The leopard gecko is a very popular pet lizard, because it is widely available and relatively easy to keep.

✳ **What is the biggest pet lizard?**
The biggest pet lizard is the green iguana, which can grow up to 1.8 metres long.

✳ **How can I find out about lizards?**
Find out about lizards in your local library. Look up a good website about lizards on the Internet, or contact a reptile society for more advice (see page 31). You could also talk to people you know who keep lizards, or ask for information at a good pet shop.

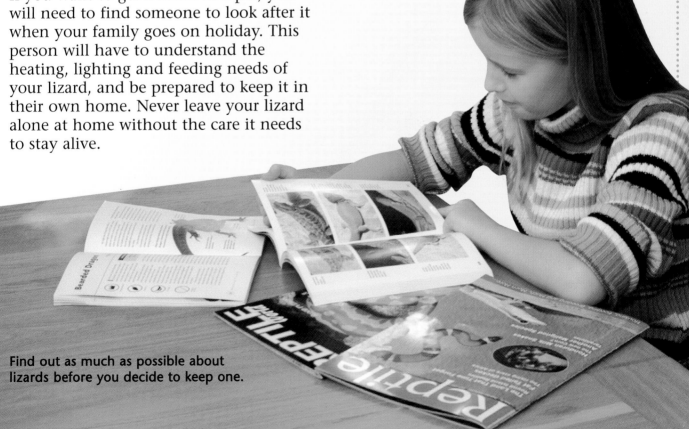

Find out as much as possible about lizards before you decide to keep one.

Choosing the right lizard

If you are new to keeping lizards, start with an easy species to look after, such as the friendly leopard gecko. Once you have more experience, you may want to take on a more challenging species, like the bearded dragon. You should wait until you are older to get a bigger, more demanding species of lizard, for example a green iguana.

Count the cost

Some lizards, such as green anoles, are not expensive to buy, but cost a lot to keep. Their living space needs to be fitted with special heating and lighting, which will have to be maintained for your lizard's lifetime. You must be sure you can afford to keep your pet lizard before you go out and buy it.

Long life

Lizards can live for a very long time – bearded dragons can live for up to ten years for example, while leopard geckos and green iguanas can live for up to 20 years. Find out how long your chosen lizard will live if it is looked after properly. Are you and your family prepared to look after it for all this time?

The green iguana needs lots of room to move and climb about.

Living space

The space you have at home for your lizard's tank will affect what kind of lizard you can choose. If you only have a small space, you will not be able to get a big lizard. Find out how big your lizard will grow. The size of its tank will depend on its adult size, the type of habitat it needs, and whether you want to keep a group together.

The right temperament

Some lizards are easier to tame than others. If you want to hold your pet lizard, you must choose a species that has the right temperament for this. When your lizard is young, you will need to spend lots of time handling it so it gets used to being held.

Skin tight

Lizards regularly shed their skin to reveal a new layer underneath. This is called 'sloughing'.

Lizard food

You must be prepared to handle the food your lizard will eat, such as live crickets or dead mice. Don't get a lizard if you don't want to feed it or watch it eat! Lizards have four different kinds of diet – they can be herbivores (plant-eaters), insectivores (insect-eaters), carnivores (meat-eaters) or omnivores (a mixture of all three diets).

Questions & Answers

✳ **Why is the leopard gecko good to keep as a pet?**
The leopard gecko is small, easy to handle and it doesn't need a lot of living space. It is a nocturnal lizard, so it doesn't require special lighting (see p.11).

✳ **Which lizards can be tamed and held?**
Of the lizards described in this book, the leopard gecko, bearded dragon and blue-tongued skink can be tamed and frequently held. The green iguana and the veiled chameleon can be held occasionally, and the green anole only very rarely.

✳ **Where is the best place to keep my lizard?**
Keep your lizard's tank indoors, away from direct sunlight, draughts and radiators. If your lizard is nocturnal, keep it in a quiet, dimly lit room where it will not be disturbed during the day and will not disturb you at night.

Bearded dragons are omnivores and have big appetites.

Lizard housing

Your lizard's tank is called a vivarium. The environment inside the vivarium should imitate your lizard's natural habitat. Add plenty of substrate (floor covering) and shelter, such as rocks, wood and plants. Remember that all lizards need humidity to help them shed their skins.

The bearded dragon likes to climb in a hot and dry environment like this one.

The right tank

Set up your vivarium a week or so before you buy your lizard, so you have time to check that everything is working properly. Buy the best container you can afford, because it has to last a long time. It should be well ventilated, with a secure top to prevent escapes. Make sure it is big enough for your lizard to grow to full adult size.

Desert ground-dwellers

Lizards that live on the ground in hot and dry conditions, such as leopard geckos, need a desert set-up in their tank. Place a heating pad at one end of the tank, under a gravel floor covering. Add logs and plants for shelter and rocks to bask on. Fix a spotlight to give light and basking heat. Spray water to provide humidity, and put drinking water in a shallow bowl.

Desert climbers

A desert set-up also suits climbing lizards like bearded dragons. Fix a full spectrum lighting tube (see p.11) and a spotlight for basking heat. Cover the floor with gravel, add rocks to bask on and plenty of climbing branches. Include an area of thick plants, spraying them with water to increase humidity. Provide a small to medium-sized water dish.

Tropical climbers

Climbing lizards that need a high level of humidity require a tropical set-up. Provide full spectrum tube lighting and a spotlight for basking. Cover the floor with gravel or woodchips, and put in plenty of tall, strong branches. Spray the vivarium frequently, and if possible, add a water feature to keep up humidity levels.

Comfort for all

If a small group of lizards is sharing a vivarium, each one will need its own basking spot, and a hiding place at both the hotter and cooler ends of the tank (see page 10).

Green anoles like to climb in a tropical environment.

Tropical ground-dwellers

Lizards that live on the ground in places of high humidity, such as blue-tongued skinks, will like a set-up that reflects this. Place a heating pad under one end of a woodchip floor, and fix a spotlight to create a basking spot. Decorate with sturdy rocks, and put leafy plants at one end to create a humid area. Spray the whole vivarium frequently. Put water in a medium-sized bowl.

This vivarium mimics the blue-tongued skink's natural habitat – a tropical forest floor.

Questions & Answers

* **Are glass or plastic tanks better?**
Glass tanks are suitable for all lizards and come in various sizes, while plastic tanks only suit smaller species that require simple heating.

* **What material should I use to line the base of my vivarium?**
Avoid material that is too fine and could harm your lizard if swallowed. The material should be absorbent, like wood chips, paper or gravel, and allow your lizard to behave naturally, to burrow for example.

* **Should I use real or false plants?**
Real plants need extra care and your pet may eat them. False plants are easy to clean, and can be realistic. Check they take your lizard's weight.

Light, heat and humidity

Lizards need enough space and the right habitat, but they also need the correct amount of heat, light and humidity. They have to rely on the temperature of their surroundings to control their body temperature. It is up to you to get this temperature right, or your lizard will become sick and may even die.

Hot and cold

In the wild, lizards move around to find hot and cold places so they can warm up or cool down. You must create both hot and cool areas in your vivarium, and control the temperature carefully. If your lizard overheats, it will lose moisture (dehydrate), and if it gets too cold, it will become sluggish and won't digest its food.

Place thermometers at each end of the vivarium, and check the temperature regularly.

Different temperatures

It is easy to create a range of temperatures in your vivarium. Place the main heat source at one end, using a thermostat to check that the tank is at the hottest temperature recommended for your species of lizard. At the other end of the tank, the temperature will be cooler, providing the variation that your lizard needs.

Heating

Use ceramic heaters or infra-red bulbs to create basking areas where your lizard can soak up heat. These heat sources don't create light, and can be controlled with a thermostat. Protect yourself and your lizard from contact with these heaters. If you use heating pads, put them under the floor covering, so they take up about half of the base area. Check them regularly as they can stop working over time.

Humidity

All lizards need humidity to help them shed their skin. However, some species, such as veiled chameleons (see page 26-7) need a very high level of humidity. Spray their vivarium with plenty of water, and ventilate it so the damp air stays fresh. Check the level of humidity with an instrument called a hygrometer.

Safety warning

Your vivarium's heating and lighting will be a fire hazard if it is not properly installed and maintained. Ask an adult to set up and check your equipment.

Lighting

The main types of lighting you need are spotlights, ordinary light bulbs and full spectrum fluorescent tube lighting. Spotlights are used to make areas of intense heat and light for basking; light bulbs also give heat and light, but have no ultraviolet (UV) content. Full-spectrum tube lighting gives UV light to help lizards stay healthy.

Questions & Answers

✴ **Do I need to time the lighting in my tank?**
Yes. All lizards need a regular 12-hour cycle of light and dark. Without this, they will suffer stress and may get ill. Remember to lower all temperatures slightly at night too, to mimic natural conditions.

✴ **Where should I put the lights in my tank?**
If your lizard needs ultraviolet light, place the light tube close to the basking light, so your lizard benefits from both when it spends time warming up.

✴ **Should I use 'hot rocks' in my vivarium?**
No. Hot rocks are false rocks fitted with a heating element to warm lizards as they rest on them. Hot rocks don't heat up the tank very well, and can burn your lizard.

In the wild, lizards use sunlight to help them digest their food. Sunlight also strengthens their bones.

Buying your lizard

When you have decided which species of lizard you want, find a good, specialist pet shop. You will need one that stocks your chosen species and supplies all its equipment and food. Get your vivarium ready and build up a store of suitable food before you buy your lizard.

Finding a good pet shop

A local vet or a national reptile society can help you find a good pet shop in your area. You could also contact a specialist reptile magazine, or do a search on the Internet with your parents. See page 31 for some suggestions on websites and contact addresses. A well-kept pet shop will sell you a healthy lizard.

Choose a clean, alert lizard.

Healthy lizards

Look for a lizard that is alert, bright-eyed, eats well and is clean. Avoid skinny, dirty or scruffy looking lizards that look uncomfortable as they walk or sit. Your lizard should breathe easily and silently, and its skin shouldn't be too wrinkled or dull.

Groups of lizards

If you want to keep a group of lizards, make sure your tank is big enough to house them all comfortably. Buy a group of females if possible, as males will fight over food and basking spots. Don't get a group of males and females, unless you want to breed them. Breeding lizards takes patience, care and skill to do properly.

12

Captive-bred

Popular species of lizards are bred in captivity. Always choose a captive-bred lizard – it will be healthier and less stressed than one that was caught in the wild and imported to the UK. It will also adapt more easily to its new home, and be easier and more hygienic to keep. It is currently still legal to import a lizard species if it is not officially endangered, but the RSPCA is campaigning to change the law. Don't support the trade in imported reptiles by buying a wild-caught lizard.

These captive-bred bearded dragons get along well together.

Questions & Answers

✳ **How do I know if a pet shop is a good one?**

A good pet shop will stock lizards that are healthy and well cared for. Its staff will know a lot about lizards, and will be able to give useful advice.

✳ **Should I buy a lizard if I feel sorry for it?**

Never buy a lizard if you feel sorry for it. It has probably been badly cared for, and buying the animal will not persuade the pet shop to improve its ways. If you see a sick lizard, tell the pet shop staff, and don't buy a lizard from that shop.

✳ **Should I buy a healthy lizard if it is kept in poor conditions?**

If you see a healthy lizard kept in poor conditions, watch out – this lizard may become ill when you get it home.

Fat tails

Lizards keep reserves of fat at the base of their tails. If a lizard has a very bony tail, it is probably not being fed properly.

Getting home

A small lizard can be transported in a ventilated plastic box, placed inside a cardboard box lined with newspaper or similar. Big lizards can be put in large cloth bags tied with string, and placed in strong wooden crates lined with polystyrene. Remember that all carrying crates or boxes should have small ventilation holes.

Feeding your lizard

Some species of lizard eat plants, some eat insects, some eat meat and some enjoy a mixture of all these different food types. Whatever kind of diet your pet lizard has, it must eat a good variety of interesting, healthy food.

Regular routine

Feed your lizard at regular times. Keep a good supply of food, and store it hygienically, in the fridge or freezer if necessary. Put your lizard's food in a stainless steel dish, placing it away from direct heat in the vivarium, so it doesn't dry out or go off. Remove uneaten food the next day, so it doesn't rot.

Water supply

Offer your lizard fresh water every day. Some species of lizard will drink from a bowl. If your lizard prefers water droplets, spray the tank regularly to allow drops to form on the leaves, rocks and branches.

Small lizards need their fruit and vegetables chopped or diced.

Fruit and vegetables

If your lizard eats fruit and vegetables, buy local, organic produce if possible, and wash it to remove any traces of pesticides. Don't cook fruit or vegetables for your lizard – it should eat everything raw. Popular vegetarian choices include spinach, cabbage, broccoli, carrot, tomato, pear, apple, berries and also some leaves, flowers and weeds, such as dandelions. Many wild plants and weeds can be poisonous to your lizard though, so always check them out with a reliable source before feeding them to your pet.

Insects

Many lizards eat insects and spiders and like to stalk their prey. Feed your lizard live insects to keep it busy and fit. Don't put too many insects in the tank at once, as the uneaten ones will pester your lizard when it has eaten enough. Your lizard will eat fruit flies, wax worms, mealworms, crickets, beetle grubs and locusts.

Your lizard will enjoy a tasty meal of grubs.

Questions & Answers

✱ **Where can I get live insects to feed my lizard?**

You can buy live insects from a supplier recommended by your pet shop. Keep your insects in good condition in ventilated plastic containers. Feed them with nutritious foods, also available from your supplier. The nutrients will be passed onto your lizard – this is called 'gut loading'.

✱ **How often should I feed my lizard?**

This depends on its species, and how old it is. Young, growing lizards need to be fed more often than older, bigger ones. Most young lizards should be fed every day, but adult lizards are usually happy with two or three good feeds a week.

✱ **Does my lizard need food supplements?**

Yes, to make sure that its diet has all the necessary vitamins and minerals. You should dust the powder over your lizard's food (even over live insects) just before you put it in the vivarium.

Wild insects

It is better not to catch wild insects to feed your lizard, as they may have eaten harmful pesticides. They could also bring unwanted pests into your vivarium.

Omnivores

Lizards that are omnivores eat meat as well as insects and plants. Every week or so, you will need to feed an omnivorous lizard a dead mouse or 'pinkie' (a bald, pink baby mouse). Store these foods hygienically in a freezer, and defrost for an hour before giving them to your lizard.

Looking after your lizard

Lizards are easy to look after if your equipment is working well. Check your vivarium's heating and lighting every day – the sooner a problem is fixed, the better for your lizard. The best way to keep your lizard healthy is to give it the right living conditions and feed it the right food.

Living alone

Most lizards are easier to look after if they are kept on their own. For example, it is much easier to check that your lizard is eating enough or shedding its skin properly if it is the only lizard in the vivarium. Lizards that are kept in a group may also fight over food and resting places.

Handling

If you handle your lizard, start when it is young. Be very careful – small lizards have delicate bones, and are easily hurt. Never pick your lizard up by its tail, or chase it to pick it up. Instead, let it climb onto your hand. Children should not handle very big lizards. Adults who handle them should wear long sleeves and strong gloves for protection.

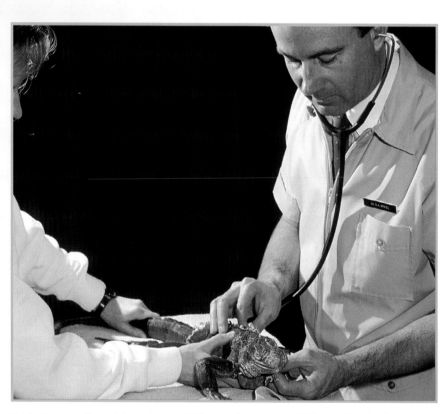

Watch your lizard for signs of illness (see page 17), and take it to the vet if something worries you.

Clean and safe

You will need to tidy your lizard's vivarium from time to time. Wear disposable plastic gloves to remove droppings when necessary. Whenever you feed and hold your lizard, or clean out its vivarium, always wash your hands afterwards. This will reduce the risk of getting, or passing on, a bacterial infection, such as salmonella.

Cleaning your vivarium

Put your lizard in a spare tank that is well heated and lit. Then unplug all your vivarium's electrical equipment. Take out the plants and decorations, throw away the substrate (floor covering) and remove the heating pads. Scrub and disinfect the tank with a suitable pet disinfectant. Rinse and dry the tank. Clean all the plants and decorations. Then put everything back in place, with fresh substrate. Finally, return your lizard to its home.

Skin problems

When lizards shed their skin, they may eat it for its nutritious value. If your lizard has problems shedding, spray the tank with extra water to increase the humidity.

Illness and old age

One common health problem for lizards is metabolic bone disease (MBD). Symptoms include bowed legs, lameness, tiredness and loss of appetite. Lizards can also suffer from parasites and get dehydrated if they don't drink enough water. Older lizards are very vulnerable to both these conditions. Always take your pet to the vet if you are worried.

Questions & Answers

✳ **How often should I clean out my vivarium?**
You will need to give the vivarium a good clean about once every two months – exactly how frequently will depend on your species of lizard.

✳ **How do I know when my lizard is shedding its skin?**
When your lizard is about to shed, its skin will start to fade. It will scratch itself and rub against things to peel off its skin. Under the old skin is a new, brighter layer.

✳ **Should I let my lizard roam free in my home?**
No, as it will be very hard to catch again, and may die if it gets outside. Always keep your lizard away from living and eating areas for hygiene and safety reasons.

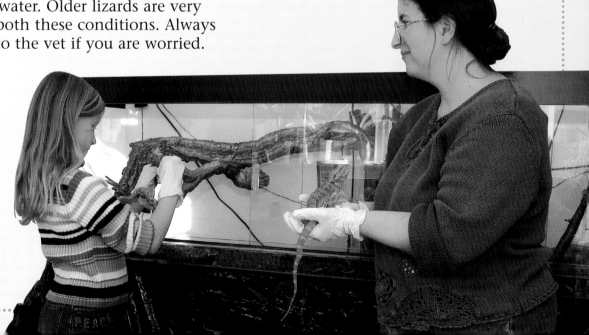

Keep a set of cleaning utensils that you only use for cleaning out your lizard's vivarium.

Leopard gecko

The leopard gecko is one of the best lizards to keep as a pet, as it has a calm temperament. It grows up to 22cm long and can live for up to 20 years. Unlike most geckos, it doesn't have sticky pads on its feet. This is because it is not a climber. The leopard gecko is also unusual because it can blink. This keeps sand out of its eyes in its natural desert habitat.

Desert home

Your leopard gecko's vivarium should measure 60cm x 30cm x 40cm (length x height x width). It doesn't have to be tall, as your lizard can't climb. You will need to create a 'desert ground-dweller' environment (see page 8). If you use sand to cover the base, use coral or cali sand, which won't harm your gecko if swallowed.

Dry, rocky desert is the natural habitat of the leopard gecko.

Insect diet

Leopard geckos eat insects – they enjoy small locusts, small to medium-sized crickets, wax worms and mealworms. An adult will eat five to six live insects each mealtime. Before you let the insects loose in the vivarium, dust them with vitamin and calcium supplements. Give your gecko fresh water every day.

Heating and lighting

Leopard geckos are nocturnal, so they don't need ultraviolet lighting during the day. Use timer switches on your lights to create a 12-hour cycle of day and night. Place heating pads under the substrate at one end of the vivarium. Use your thermostat to get a daytime temperature of 32°C at the hot end, and 26°C at the cool end. At night, don't let the temperature drop below 21°C.

Hold young leopard geckos every day for a short time. They will soon become tame.

Questions & Answers

✱ **How often should I feed my leopard gecko?**

Feed young leopard geckos once a day. Adult leopard geckos only need feeding every other day. A well-fed adult gecko with a plump tail can actually survive without food for a whole week – but don't put this to the test.

✱ **How can I make my leopard gecko's vivarium humid?**

Place a box of plastic plants at the hot end of your vivarium, and spray it with water every day to create humidity. This will stop your lizard from getting dehydrated, and help it to shed skin.

✱ **How should I hold my leopard gecko?**

Pick it up by placing one hand flat on top of its body, holding its neck gently between your finger and thumb. Slide your other hand underneath its body to support its legs. Sit down with your lizard, and cup it carefully in your hands. Wash your hands after you put it back.

Keeping clean

Leopard geckos are clean and tidy lizards. They use one part of the vivarium as a toilet – you will have to remove droppings from this area every other day or so. Wear disposable gloves to do this. Give your whole vivarium a thorough clean once every three months. Always wash your hands afterwards.

What big eyes you have…

Leopard geckos have huge eyes, which help them see and hunt in the dark.

Telling tails

Never pick up your gecko by its tail. It may drop off, as this is how geckos escape from attackers when caught in the wild. Amazingly, the tail will grow back, but it will be shorter and stumpier than before.

Bearded dragon

The omnivorous bearded dragon comes from the hot desert and dry woodland of Australia. This lizard has a gentle temperament and can be tamed. However, it is a challenging and expensive pet to look after. Bearded dragons grow to full size – up to 60cm long – in just one year, and live for about 12 years.

Setting up

Bearded dragons are active lizards and need lots of space. A female pair will require a tank measuring at least 150cm x 50cm x 50cm (length x height x width). The vivarium should have a 'desert climber' set-up (see page 8). Use coral sand or bark chips as substrate. Place cork logs and rocks at both ends for shelter and basking spots. Make sure all climbing branches are strong and sturdy.

Natural conditions

Set up a 12-hour cycle of heating and light. Daytime temperatures should range between 28 to 40°C, dropping to 20°C at night. Place a heating pad at one end and fix full spectrum fluorescent tubes to give ultraviolet light. Create basking areas with spotlights and spray the tank regularly with water.

Big eaters

Bearded dragons are omnivorous and have healthy appetites, eating insects, plants and meat. Their diet should be approximately 60% insects, 30% plants and 10% meat. Give your lizard plenty of live insects to catch. Offer chopped green vegetables and fruit, and the occasional pinkie mouse. Give your lizard fresh water every day in a shallow dish.

Your bearded dragon should have a healthy, mixed diet.

Clearing up the mess

The bearded dragon is a burrower, and makes a mess when it digs. It eats a lot, so produces lots of waste. You must remove droppings and take away leftover food every day. Wipe down the vivarium once a week, and do a thorough clean once a month. Wear disposable gloves and wash your hands afterwards.

What's in a name?

The bearded dragon gets its name from the skin flap under its chin, and the soft, dragon-like spines along its body.

Pecking order

If you keep more than one bearded dragon one of them will become dominant, always feeding and choosing its basking spot first. Check that all your lizards are eating enough and watch out for aggression or bullying.

Questions & Answers

✳ Where should I put the lighting in my vivarium?
Place your full spectrum lighting tube close to a spotlight, so your bearded dragon gets the ultraviolet light it needs while it basks in the heat.

✳ How often should I feed my bearded dragon?
Young 'beardies' eat more meat than adults, and should be fed every day. Feed fully-grown adults four or five times a week. Wait until the tank has warmed up to feed your lizards, as the heat helps them digest their food.

✳ How should I hold my bearded dragon?
Pick up your bearded dragon gently, scooping it up with the palm of your hand and curling your fingers over its body. Never pick it up by its tail, and don't try to grab it. If your lizard has long claws, get them clipped by a vet so they don't scratch you.

Bearded dragons puff out their throats when they are threatened, and make their spines stand up. They also flatten themselves to appear bigger and broader.

Blue-tongued skink

Skinks are smooth-scaled lizards that live mainly in temperate and tropical areas. Like all skinks, the blue-tongued skink has a long, flat body and short legs. This Australian lizard can grow up to 60cm long and lives for up to ten years. It is active at dawn and dusk.

Tropical tank

The blue-tongued skink needs a tank of at least 150cm x 90cm x 30cm (length x height x width). A tank with a removable roof is best, as sliding doors are not appropriate for this burrowing lizard. Use plenty of cali or coral sand, woodchips or aspen bedding for the substrate. Add some flat, mossy rocks. Don't plant delicate plants, as this lizard will uproot them. Your vivarium should have a 'tropical ground-dweller' set-up (see page 9).

This fascinating lizard sticks out its bright blue tongue to frighten predators away.

Hiding places

Give your blue-tongued skink plenty of hiding places, for example PVC pipes. There should be lots of shelter at the hotter and cooler ends of the vivarium. Secure all your wood pieces and rocks so they don't topple over when your lizard starts burrowing.

Heat, light and humidity

The blue-tongued skink needs a daytime temperature of 25–35°C, and a night temperature of 18–20°C. Put a heating pad under one end of the substrate, and create a basking area with a spotlight. Your lizard will need full spectrum ultraviolet lighting. Put some moss in one corner and spray it daily with water to keep up the humidity.

Varied diet

This lizard is an omnivore and eats meat, insects and plants. It enjoys dog or cat food mixed with fresh fruit, such as banana or pear. An occasional pinkie mouse is also welcome. Insect treats could include crickets, wax worms and mealworms. Flowers, for example roses and carnations, are a tasty alternative to green vegetables.

Baby blues

Unlike most lizards, blue-tongued skinks don't lay eggs, but give birth to live young.

Water and cleaning

Give your lizard water in a sturdy bowl and change it every day. The bowl may need to be cleaned when you change the water, because this skink sometimes uses its bowl as a toilet! You should clean out your vivarium about once a month.

Questions & Answers

✳ **How often should I feed my blue-tongued skink?**
When your blue-tongued skink is under six months old, feed it every day. Older skinks can be fed every two or three days. Add calcium and vitamin supplements to the food – do this daily for young lizards and twice a week for adults.

✳ **How should I hold my blue-tongued skink?**
Pick it up gently, letting it sit on your hand and along your arm. Hold the back of its head with your fingers and use your other hand to hold the base of its tail and back legs. Adult blue-tongued skinks have strong jaws and sharp teeth, so if your lizard doesn't want to be held, leave it alone.

✳ **Will my blue-tongued skink shed its skin?**
Yes, but sometimes blue-tongued skinks have problems shedding all of it. You may have to get a vet to remove any unshed skin.

The blue-tongued skink should have a very varied diet.

Green anole

The green anole is also called the American chameleon because it can change the colour of its skin from green to brown – but this only happens if it is very stressed. Active during the day, this lively and entertaining lizard comes from southern USA, Central America and the Caribbean. It grows up to 20cm long and lives for three to five years.

The green anole shows off its bright orange skin flap in head-bobbing displays.

Feeding time

Green anoles eat insects. Offer a good variety, but make sure your pet's head is at least twice as big as each offering, or it may not be able to catch or eat it. Dust your insects with vitamin and mineral supplements for extra nutrition. Feed adults every other day, making sure each lizard eats about two insects. If one of your lizards is not eating enough, you may have to feed it in a separate tank for a while.

Tropical climber

You may want to keep a group of green anoles together. Four green anoles should have a tank of at least 90cm x 60cm x 30cm (length x height x width). They need a tall living space because they are acrobatic climbers. Provide a 'tropical climber' set-up (see page 9), with plenty of plants for climbing on and hiding behind.

Temperature

Green anoles need ultraviolet light from full spectrum tube lighting. You should also provide enough spotlights for each of your anoles to have a basking place. The temperature should be between 23°C and 30°C during the day, dropping to around 20°C at night.

Water and humidity

Green anoles drink water droplets on plants, and won't drink from a bowl. Your vivarium needs to be very humid so water droplets can form. Try to keep the humidity level at about 60–70%, so your lizards have enough to drink. Check humidity with your hygrometer.

Any other anoles?

There are over 300 species of anole, but the green anole is the kind most often kept as a pet.

Nervous type

Green anoles are difficult to handle. If you need to catch a green anole, don't chase it. Offer a treat, such as a wax worm, on your hand and wait for your lizard to come to get it. Keep calm and still, and gently cup the lizard in your hands. Always wash your hands after holding your lizard.

Questions & Answers

✳ **Should I get a group of males or females?**
Females are easier to look after. A small group of females of the same size and age will get on better than a group of males, with less competition for territory.

✳ **Will my anole lose its tail?**
Yes, but only if you try to catch it by grabbing its tail. Never do this, as it will cause great distress to your pet.

✳ **What kind of plants should I put in my vivarium?**
Real plants are best, to help keep up humidity. The green anole is an insectivore, so it will not eat the plants in its vivarium. Try tropical houseplants such as bromeliads, ivy and vines. Your plants must be strong enough to take the weight of your lizards.

Spray your plants with water every day, to keep up the humidity in your vivarium.

Veiled chameleon

The veiled chameleon of southwestern Asia is a commonly kept chameleon, but it is not a good lizard for beginners. It is tricky to look after, and can easily become stressed and sick. Healthy veiled chameleons grow up to 60cm long, and can live for up to eight years.

Distinguishing features

The veiled chameleon changes colour to blend in with its surroundings, control its body temperature and communicate. Its eyes move separately, which helps it judge distances. It uses its long tongue to snap up insects. Opposing toes and a strong tail help it to grip branches.

This chameleon's tongue is up to one and a half times longer than its body.

Leafy home

The veiled chameleon needs a large, tall tank, measuring at least 92cm x 92cm x 51cm (length x height x width). It is best to keep this lizard on its own as pairs (particularly males) can be very aggressive towards each other. Your vivarium should have a 'desert climber' set-up (see page 8), with strong leafy branches filling up most of the space. Make sure your plants are non-toxic, and don't use fine sand as a substrate as it could harm your chameleon.

Heat and light

Your chameleon will need full spectrum lighting to get the ultraviolet light it needs. Create at least two basking areas in the vivarium, using spotlights. The 'hot' end of your vivarium should be about 30°C, and the 'cool' end should be about 20°C. At night the temperature should not drop below 16°C.

Start holding your veiled chameleon when it is young, so it will get used to you. Don't handle it too often, as this will stress your pet.

Questions & Answers

* **How do I know if my chameleon is stressed?**

Your chameleon will go dark brown or black and stop eating if it gets stressed. It could be upset by having the wrong living conditions, or by too much movement and noise. Put your vivarium in a quiet place, and move slowly when you go near it.

* **How humid should my veiled chameleon's vivarium be?**

Your vivarium needs to have a high level of humidity, so spray it regularly with water or install a drip system. These are available from good reptile pet shops.

* **How do I let my chameleon get used to me?**

Try getting your chameleon to take a tasty treat, such as a wax worm, from your hand when it is about ten weeks old.

Healthy eating

Veiled chameleons are omnivores – they will eat insects, plants and meat. They prefer to catch climbing and flying insects, such as crickets and wax moths. Dust these with vitamin and mineral supplements before you put them in the vivarium. Veiled chameleons eat a range of fruit and vegetables. Once a week or so, a pinkie mouse will also go down well.

Boy power

Male veiled chameleons are easier to keep than females. They are bigger, stronger and less fussy about food.

Water drops

Veiled chameleons drink water drops on plants. They drink a lot, so you will have to either spray water over the vivarium plants twice a day to create enough drops, or install a drip system. Keep the tank well ventilated so that the damp air stays fresh.

Green iguana

The green iguana comes from Central and South America. This large, active lizard is not a good choice for beginners. It grows up to 1.8 metres long, and lives for 10 to 15 years. As it gets older and bigger, it can become aggressive and hard to look after. Before you buy a green iguana, you must be certain that you and your family have enough space and time to keep it.

Think big

Get an adult-sized vivarium for a young green iguana so it has enough space to grow. An adult green iguana needs a very big vivarium, measuring at least 2m x 1.8m x 1.2m (length x height x width). You may have to get a tank made, or convert a small room into a vivarium with sliding double-glazed doors.

The green iguana climbs, runs and swims in its tropical rainforest habitat.

Leafy home

Line the base of your iguana's vivarium with woodchips, leaf litter or pebbles. Create a 'tropical climber' set-up (see page 9). Provide strong logs for climbing and plastic plants for shade (your iguana will eat real plants). Supply plenty of hiding places, for example with large pieces of cork log.

Heating and lighting

Your green iguana needs full spectrum fluorescent lighting. Set your lights to a 12-hour cycle of night and day, creating daytime basking areas with spotlights. Temperatures should range between 25°C and 30°C, dropping to about 24°C at night. Spray the vivarium with water every other day to increase humidity.

Adult green iguanas should be handled with great care.

Plant power

Adult green iguanas are herbivorous, meaning they only eat plants, but as they are so big they need a lot of them! Provide a nutritious mixture of fruit, leaves and vegetables in a strong, non-spillable bowl. Young iguanas need their food chopped, and will also eat some live foods, such as crickets, locust hoppers and wax worms.

Questions & Answers

✴ **How often should I feed my green iguana?**
Feed your green iguana every other day. Remove uneaten food the day after you offered it. Give fresh water every day in a clean, sturdy bowl.

✴ **How can I tame my green iguana?**
Start to tame your iguana when you first get it. Let it get used to you by hand-feeding it regularly. To pick up a green iguana, hold it behind its neck and above its rear legs, tucking the long tail under your arm. Wait until you are big and strong enough to hold an adult!

✴ **How will I know if my green iguana's claws are too long?**
Your green iguana's claws are too long if they look like they could scratch you. Take your lizard to the vet to have them trimmed, or they could inflict a nasty injury.

Boy or girl?

It can be hard to tell the sex of young green iguanas. From about the age of three, males grow a crest of spines down their backs, and a large flap of skin under their jaws.

Take care

Be careful handling your green iguana when it is small. Frightened baby green iguanas can 'drop' or lose their tails in self-defence. Green iguanas may become aggressive as they get older and bigger. Children should not even try to hold adult green iguanas.

Glossary

Absorbent
Able to absorb or soak up liquid.

Bask
To absorb heat and ultraviolet rays from the sun (or from another strong source of heat and light).

Captive-bred
An animal that has been bred in captivity, and has never lived in its natural environment.

Carnivore
An animal that eats only or mainly meat.

Cold-blooded
Animals that rely on the temperature of their surroundings to control their body temperature.

Dehydrated
Having lost vital body moisture.

Full spectrum fluorescent lighting
Full spectrum fluorescent lighting gives out ultraviolet (UV) light.

Gut loading
Feeding lizards with insects that were well fed with healthy foods.

Habitat
Where an animal lives in the wild, such as a desert or tropical rainforest.

Herbivore
An animal that eats plants.

Humidity
Moisture in the air.

Hygrometer
An instrument used to check the level of humidity in a vivarium.

Insectivore
An animal that eats insects. Insects are part or all of most lizards' diet.

Nocturnal
Awake and active during the night.

Omnivore
Lizards that are omnivores have a diet that includes plants, insects and meat.

Parasites
Tiny creatures that feed on the animal they live on or in.

Pesticides
Chemicals used to kill pests, such as insects or rodents.

Predators
Animals that eat other animals.

Reptile
A scaly, cold-blooded animal.

Substrate
A thick layer of loose material that lines the base of a vivarium.

Temperate
A mild climate, neither hot nor cold.

Thermostat
A device that keeps temperatures steady. A thermostat can be adjusted to allow the temperature to become hotter or cooler.

Tropical
From a hot place close to the equator.

Ultraviolet (UV) light
Light rays that help lizards' bones to grow, and are good for their health.

Vivarium
A tank.

Useful websites

If you want to learn more about types of lizards, buying lizards, looking after lizards, or if you would like to get involved in animal welfare, these are some helpful websites:

UNITED KINGDOM
Royal Society for the Prevention of Cruelty to Animals (RSPCA)
A campaigning charity for animals and useful source of advice on keeping lizards.
Website: www.rspca.org.uk
Contact address:
Enquiries service, RSPCA, Wilberforce Way, Southwater, Horsham, West Sussex, United Kingdom RH13 9RS.
Tel: 0870 33 35 999

The Federation of British Herpetologists
This organisation promotes and supports the responsible keeping of reptiles and amphibians by people in the UK.
Website: www.f-b-h.co.uk
Email: enquiries@f-b-h.co.uk

The British Herpetological Society
This society organises conservation activities, particularly for British species of amphibians and reptiles. It is open to scientists, conservationists and all reptile enthusiasts.
Website: www.thebhs.org
Email: info@thebhs.org
Contact address:
The British Herpetological Society, 11, Strathmore Place, Montrose, Angus, United Kingdom DD10 8LQ

The Reptile Experience
A family-run company that offers tips and advice on caring for reptiles, as well as a rescue service.
Website: www.reptilehouse.net

AUSTRALIA
Australian Herpetological Society
Society devoted to reptiles.
Website: www.ahs.org.au
Email: webmaster@ahs.org.au

Aussie Reptile Keeper
Good Australian website with useful information about keeping reptiles.
Website: www.aussiereptilekeeper.com

UNITED STATES OF AMERICA
American Society of Ichthyologists and Herpetologists
This academic society focuses on the scientific study of reptiles, fish, amphibians, turtles and crocodilians
Website: www.asih.org

INTERNATIONAL
The International Herpetological Society
Subscribe to become a member of this organisation and receive regular newsletters and a reptile journal. There are lots of local branches of this society.
Website: www.international-herpetological-society.org

Note to parents and teachers:
Every effort has been made by the Publishers to ensure that these websites are suitable for children, that they are of the highest educational value, and that they contain no inappropriate or offensive material. However, because of the nature of the Internet, it is impossible to guarantee that the contents of these sites will not be altered. We strongly advise that Internet access is supervised by a responsible adult.

Index